7106

Mel Bay presents

DULCIMER JAM

Favorite Jam Session Tunes Arranged for:

Hammered Dulcimer

Fretted Dulcimer

Guitar

Other melodic and chorded Instruments

By Bonnie Carol

Book layout, design, and computer musical notation © Bonnie Carol, 2003. I love sharing music. Please get in touch to arrange use of this material. Bonnie@BonnieCarol.com
www.BonnieCarol.com • (303) 258-7763 • 15 Sherwood Road • Nederland, Colorado 80466

I have made every effort to trace copyright owners, but to anyone who feels that their right has been infringed upon, I express my sincere regret, and I request that you contact me so I can correct the situation.

Library of Congress Control Number: 2002091990

1 2 3 4 5 6 7 8 9 0

Visit us on the Web at www.melbay.com — E-mail us at email@melbay.com

Contents

*(*4) – Songs arranged for four equidistant strings on Fretted Dulcimer*

Thanks . . .

My students contribute immeasurably to this book. I write this music out for them, and they carefully learn to play what is written ... even the mistakes. In this way, they are my editors extraordinaire. And beyond the call of duty is the stellar editing by Penny Bauer, Holly Beazley, and Donna Lewin.

Introduction

As I've taught music over the last two decades, I've found that many adults study music because they want to be part of those wonderful jams that happen any time two or more musicians are gathered. It's true there's nothing more fun, and that is the purpose of this book – to give a variety of songs that are arranged so players of hammered and fretted dulcimers, guitars, flutes, mandolins, pianos, or whistles who read melody lines, guitar chords, or fretted dulcimer tablature can learn songs together. I recommend getting together with some friends, eating a potluck supper, learning some of these tunes and arrangements, and having a DULCIMER JAM SESSION!

Using the Music in this Book

Some of the pieces are simple, others more difficult. The order of the book goes roughly from easier to more difficult tunes. All the tunes are arranged for hammered and fretted dulcimers and all have standard music notation and chord notation. Some are written for fretted dulcimers with four equidistant strings, but most are for three course dulcimers. There are pieces which are meant to be fingerpicked, others which are meant to be strummed, and still others that I thought a single note flatpicking approach was appropriate. Some of the hammered dulcimer arrangements include embellishments, and others are left with a simple melody line so you can make your own arrangements. A few pieces have several different arrangements to choose from or are arranged as duets. I hope you can learn something about a variety of arranging ideas from the different treatments of the various pieces. If you need more instruction, try DUST OFF THAT DULCIMER AND DANCE: A MOUNTAIN DULCIMER INSTRUCTION BOOK, available from Bonnie Carol, 15 Sherwood Road, Nederland, Colorado, 80466. I am also happy to receive corrections, comments, and correspondence about this work at that address. The purpose of music is to learn it and share it, and then make it your own in the process. Use these arrangements for guidelines, and add your own ideas to the soup. I can't wait to see what you do with these tunes!

About the Author

That's me, Bonnie Carol. I began teaching dulcimer almost as soon as I learned to play it, and through those first years teaching, I came to understand my own informal musical education better and how to communicate it to others. I played piano from the time I could walk, accompanying community theater and school choirs till I went to college and discovered the guitar and folk music. When I was twenty-five, Max Krimmel made a fretted dulcimer for me, and I cobbled together enough information to make some sense of the modes and tunings, and off I went – learning to play. I began doing everything dulcimer – I built dulcimers, I taught dulcimer, I made dulcimer recordings, I wrote dulcimer books, and I performed on dulcimer. In 1979, Dana Hamilton offered to trade me a hammered dulcimer he made for a fretted dulcimer I made, and thus began the study of new instruments for both of us. Dana won honors in various fretted dulcimer contests at about the same time I did so with his hammered dulcimer. This was the genesis of this book for both dulcimers.

Frère Jacques ~ in DAD and DAA Tunings

French Round

With these two arrangements of "Frère Jacques" you can compare the DAD and the DAA tunings of the fretted dulcimer. The chords never change in "Frère Jacques" - the only chord is a D.

Key of D
Ionian Melody
Tune D A DD
Strummed

Arrangement for Dulcimers © Bonnie Carol 2002

♩ = 132

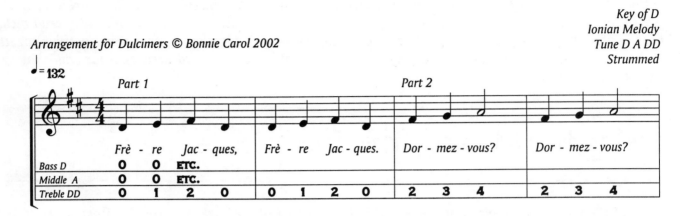

	Part 1								Part 2							
	Frè - re		Jac - ques,		Frè - re		Jac - ques.		Dor - mez - vous?			Dor - mez - vous?			
Bass D	0	0	ETC.												
Middle A	0	0	ETC.												
Treble DD	0	1	2	0	0	1	2	0	2	3	4	2	3	4	

Part 3						Part 4						
Son-nez les ma - ti - nes.						Son-nez les ma - ti - nes.						Din din don, din din don.
4 5 4 3 2 0						4 5 4 3 2 0						0 0 0 0

Key of D
Ionian Melody
Tune D A AA
Strummed

	Part 1								Part 2							
	Frè - re		Jac - ques,		Frè - re		Jac - ques.		Dor - mez - vous?			Dor - me - vous?			
Bass D	0	0	ETC.												
Middle A	0	0	ETC.												
Treble AA	3	4	5	3	3	4	5	3	5	6	7	5	6	7	

Part 3						Part 4						
Son-nez les ma - ti - nes.						Son-nez les ma - ti - nes.						Din din don, Din din don.
7 8 7 6 5 3						7 8 7 6 5 3						3 0 3 3 0 3

Bonnie@BonnieCarol.com • www.BonnieCarol.com • (303) 258-7763 • 15 Sherwood Road • Nederland, Colorado 80466

Dear Friends, Dear Friends

Four Part Round

A round has a number of parts, all parts playing the same melody but beginning at different times. Harmonically speaking, the reason rounds work is either that they don't change chords at all, or that all phrases have the same chord structure. This insures that the phrases can be sung simultaneously. In "Frère Jacques," the chords don't change at all, and in "Dear Friends," the chords change according to the same pattern in all phrases.

Key of Dm
Aeolian or Dorian mode
Tune D A GG
Strummed

Arrangement for Dulcimers © Bonnie Carol, 1996

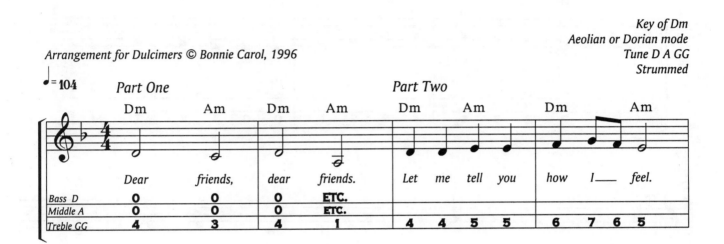

Some other sets of words that use the same melody:

Rose, Rose, Rose, Rose,
Will I ever see thee wed?
I will marry at thy will, sire,
At thy will.

Peace, peace, peace, peace.
Wars have been and wars must cease.
We must learn to live together.
Peace, peace, peace.

Love, love, love, love.
People, we are made for love.
Love thy neighbor as thy brother.
Love, love, love.

Bonnie@BonnieCarol.com • www.BonnieCarol.com • (303) 258-7763 • 15 Sherwood Road • Nederland, CO 80466

Ode to Joy

By Ludwig van Beethoven

Arrangement for Dulcimers © Bonnie Carol 2002

Key of D
Ionian Melody
Tune D A DD
Strummed

♩=130

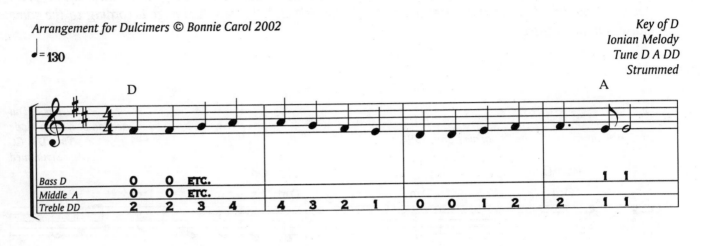

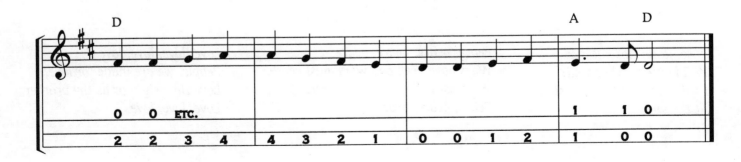

Bonnie@BonnieCarol.com • www.BonnieCarol.com • (303) 258-7763 • 15 Sherwood Road • Nederland, Colorado 80466

Oh, How Lovely Is the Evening

Traditional American Round

Arrangement for Dulcimers © Bonnie Carol 2002

Key of D
Ionian Melody
Tune D A D D
Strummed

♩.= 76

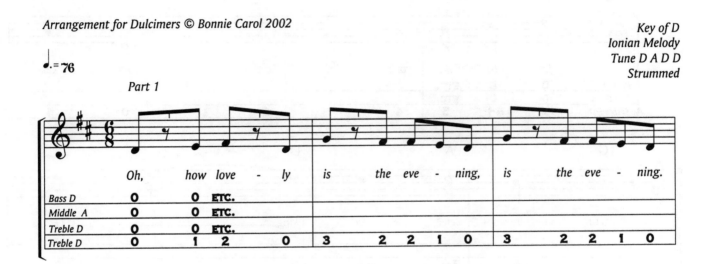

Part 1

Oh,   how   love - ly   is   the   eve - ning,   is   the   eve - ning.

Bass D	0		0	ETC.								
Middle A	0		0	ETC.								
Treble D	0		0	ETC.								
Treble D	0	1	2		0	3	2	2	1	0	3	2 2 1 0

Part 2

Bells   of   peace   are   sweet - ly   ring - ing,   sweet - ly   ring - ing.

2	3	4	2	5	4 4 3 2	5	4 4 3	2

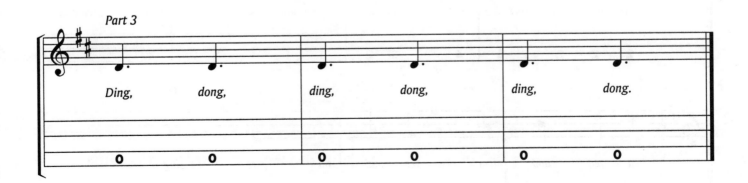

Part 3

Ding,   dong,   ding,   dong,   ding,   dong.

0	0	0	0	0	0

Bonnie@BonnieCarol.com • www.BonnieCarol.com • (303) 258-7763 • 15 Sherwood Road • Nederland, Colorado 80466

Joy to the World ~ Melody Version

Key of D
Ionian Melody
Tune D A DD
Strummed

Arrangement for Dulcimers © Bonnie Carol 2001

Bonnie@BonnieCarol.com • www.BonnieCarol.com • (303) 258-7763 • 15 Sherwood Road • Nederland, Colorado 80466

Joy to the World ~ Chorded Version

Christmas Carol
By George Frederic Handel

Arrangement for Dulcimers © Bonnie Carol 2001

*Key of D
Ionian Melody
Tune D A DD
Strummed*

Scotland the Brave

Traditional Scottish March

This is the most well known of the Scottish bagpipe marches and can be heard hundreds of times during the weekends of the Scottish Games. I tune the fretted dulcimer D D DD, with the middle string matching the two trebles. Then I play in the key of G, fretting only the melody string and not changing chords which gives me a prominent drone on the fifth of the G scale, the D note. This mimics the sound of the bagpipe drones.

Arrangement for Dulcimers © Bonnie Carol 2001

Key of G
Ionian Melody
Tune D D DD
Strummed

Bonnie@BonnieCarol.com • www.BonnieCarol.com • (303) 258-7763 • 15 Sherwood Road • Nederland, Colorado 80466

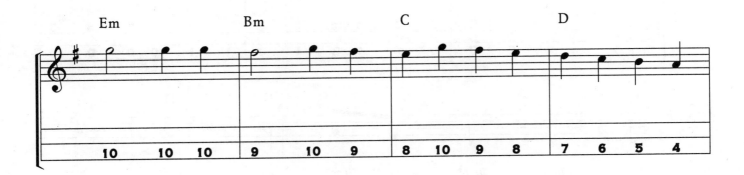

Loch Lomond

Traditional Scottish Song

This is likely the most well-known Scottish folk song. By tuning D D DD, you get a decidedly bagpipe feel which fits this Scottish piece perfectly.

Arrangement for Dulcimers © Bonnie Carol 2003

Key of D
Ionian Melody
Tune D D DD
Strummed

Twas there that we parted in yon shady glen
On the steep, steep side o' Ben Lomond,
Where in purple hue the Highland hills we view,
And the morn shines out from the gloaming.

The wee bird may sing and the wild flowers spring
And in sunshine the waters are sleeping;
But the broken heart will know no second spring again,
And the world does not know how we're grieving.

Bonnie@BonnieCarol.com • www.BonnieCarol.com • (303) 258-7763 • 15 Sherwood Road • Nederland, Colorado 80466

Wayfaring Stranger

Traditional American Hymn

This fretted dulcimer tablature is for a four-course fretted dulcimer. If yours is a three-course one, just omit the notes played on the inner treble string. (Most of these notes on the inner treble string are unfretted in any case). Strum all the strings, changing chords only when a new chord is noted in the tablature number.

Key of Bm
Aeolian Melody
Tune E A A A, capo 1st Fret
Strummed

Arrangement for Dulcimers © Bonnie Carol 2001

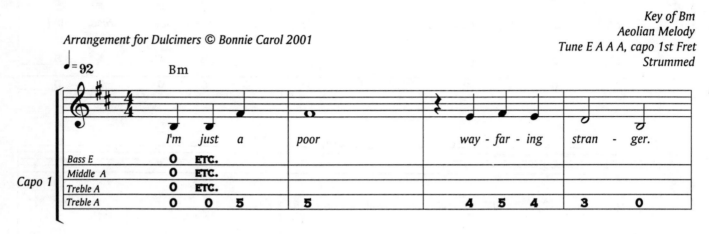

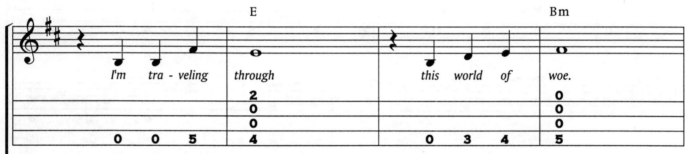

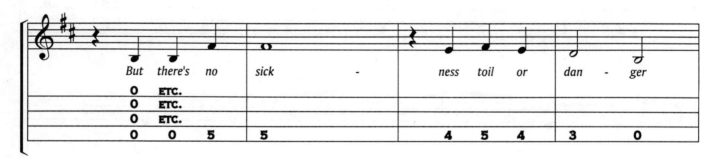

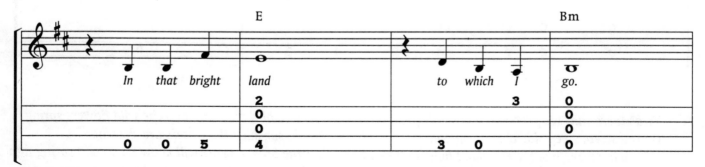

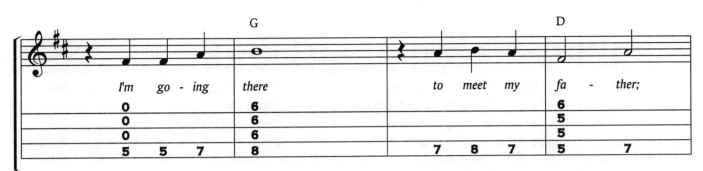

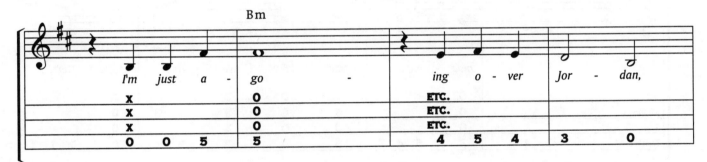

I know dark clouds will gather round me,	*I want to wear a crown of glory,*
I know my way is steep and rough,	*When I get home to that bright land.*
But beauteous fields lie just beyond me,	*I want to shout Salvation's story,*
Where souls redeemed their vigil keep.	*In concert with that bloodwashed band.*
I'm going there to meet my mother.	*I'm going there to meet my saviour,*
She said she'd meet me when I come.	*To sing his praise forever more.*
I'm only going over Jordan,	*I'm only going over Jordan,*
I'm only going over home.	*I'm only going over home.*

Amazing Grace - Key of G

Words: John Newton (1725-1807)
Music: Traditional

I read in RISE UP SINGING, the definitive catalog of words to American folk song published by SING OUT MAGAZINE, "John Newton was the captain of a slaveship who experienced a religious conversion en route to America, turned his ship around and returned to Africa, freeing his human cargo." This arrangement is for hammered dulcimer and four-course fretted dulcimer. If your fretted dulcimer is a three-course one, you can simply ignore the inner treble string notation. Play this arrangement with a flatpick, picking only the strings which have tablature numbers. On the hammered dulcimer you may make the arrangement a bit more interesting by adding notes from the guitar chord notation. In other words, when a G chord is called for, play a G, B, or D harmony note (preferably a different note than the melody plays).

Key of G
Ionian Melody
Tune D G D D
Flatpicked

Arrangement for Dulcimers © Tina Adcock and Bonnie Carol 2001

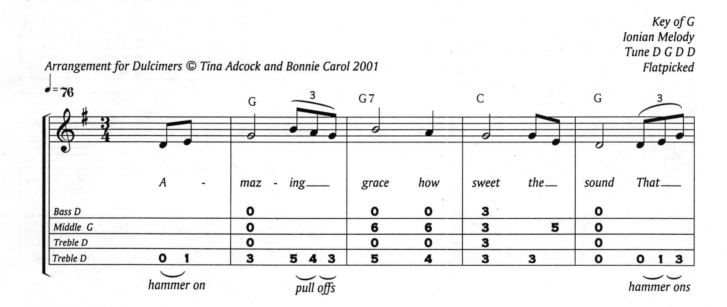

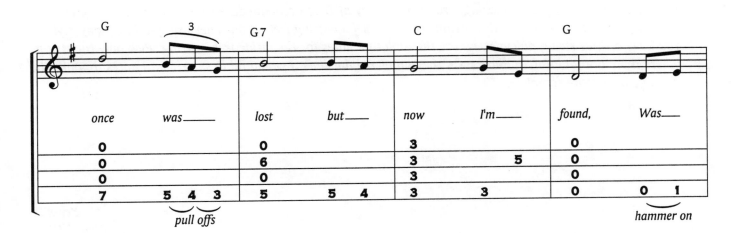

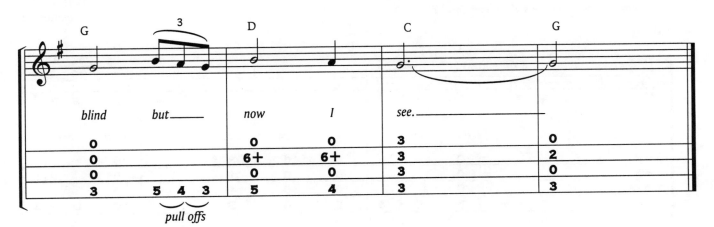

Amazing Grace! How sweet the sound
That saved a wretch like me.
I once was lost but now I'm found,
Was blind but now I see.

'Twas grace that taught my heart to fear
And grace my fears relieved.
How precious did that grace appear
The hour I first believed.

The Lord has promised good to me.
His word my hope secures.
He will my shield and portion be
As long as life endures.

Through many dangers, toils, and snares
I have already come.
'Tis grace that brought me safe thus far
And grace will lead me home.

Amazing Grace - Key of D

Words: John Newton (1725-1807)
Music: Traditional

You might choose to play "Amazing Grace" in the key of D to accommodate singers with lower voices than the key of G called for. Again, this arrangement is for four-string fretted dulcimer using a flatpicking style. If you have a three string dulcimer, ignore the tablature notes for the inside treble string. Pick only the strings where there are tablature numbers. On the hammered dulcimer, I would fill in some chord notes to make the arrangement more complete.

Key of D
Ionian Melody
Tune D A A A
Flatpicked

Arrangement for Dulcimers © Bonnie Carol 2001

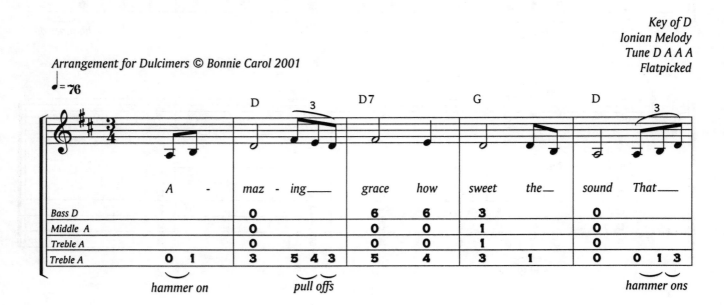

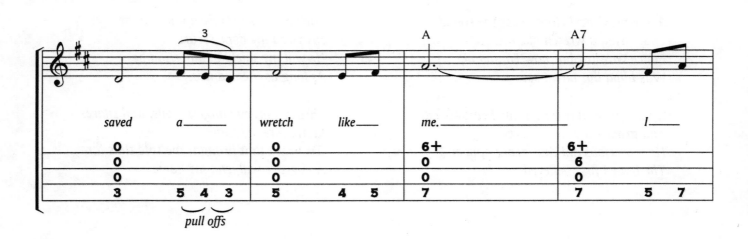

Bonnie@BonnieCarol.com • www.BonnieCarol.com • (303) 258-7763 • 15 Sherwood Road • Nederland, Colorado 80466

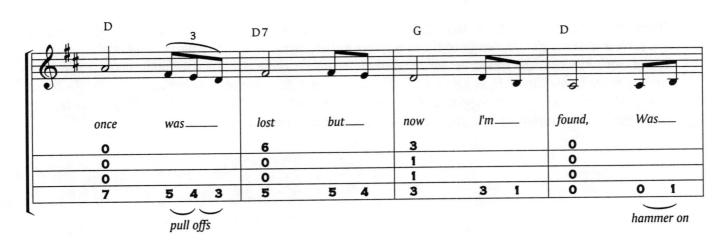

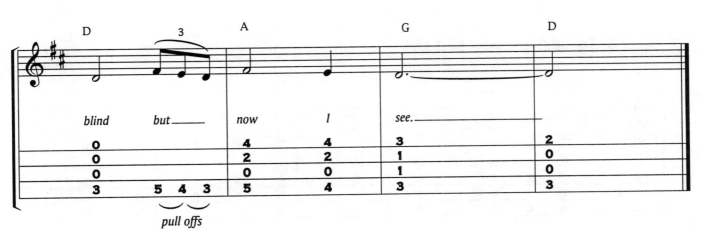

Amazing Grace! How sweet the sound
That saved a wretch like me.
I once was lost but now I'm found,
Was blind but now I see.

'Twas grace that taught my heart to fear
And grace my fears relieved.
How precious did that grace appear
The hour I first believed.

The Lord has promised good to me.
His word my hope secures.
He will my shield and portion be
As long as life endures.

Through many dangers, toils, and snares
I have already come.
'Tis grace that brought me safe thus far
And grace will lead me home.

Bonnie@BonnieCarol.com • www.BonnieCarol.com • (303) 258-7763 • 15 Sherwood Road • Nederland, Colorado 80466

Dona Nobis Pacem

Three Part Round

"Dona Nobis Pacem" translates from Latin to "Grant Us Peace." This is a round with an eight measure cycle. Note that the chords change in the same place in the phrases in all three parts; that is what makes a round work harmonically speaking. For the fretted dulcimer, I chose the D A AA tuning because there are melody notes below the tonic, in this case, a D. Those lower notes are available in this tuning on the treble string. Note the rolling or arpeggiated chord symbol in the hammered dulcimer music. Play the notes one at a time quickly, beginning with the lowest and going to the highest.

Key of D
Ionian Mode
Tune D A AA
Strummed

Arrangement for Dulcimers © Bonnie Carol, 1996

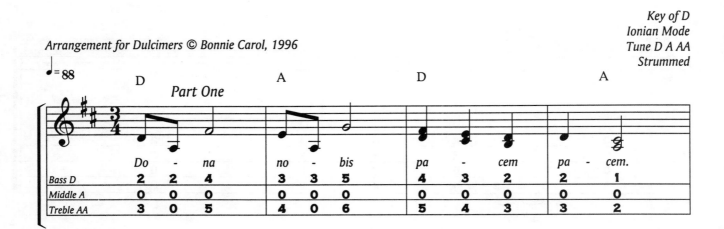

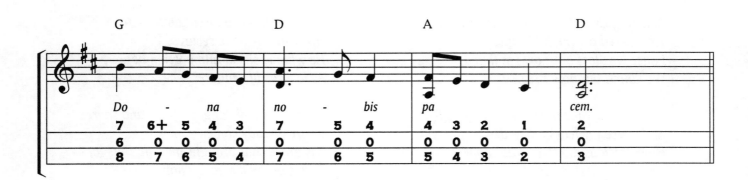

Bonnie@BonnieCarol.com • www.BonnieCarol.com • (303) 258-7763 • 15 Sherwood Road • Nederland, Colorado 80466

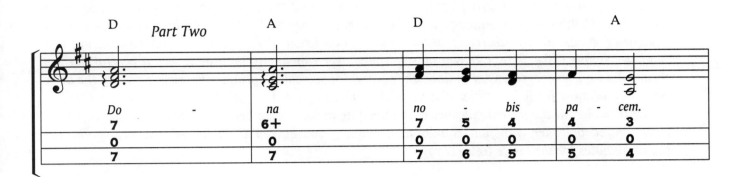

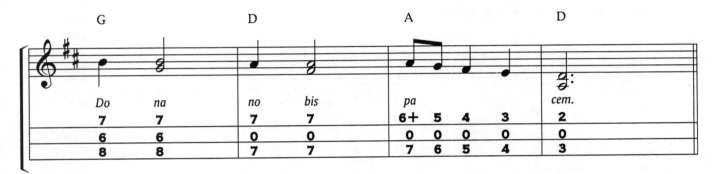

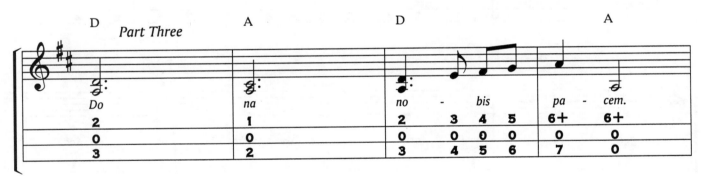

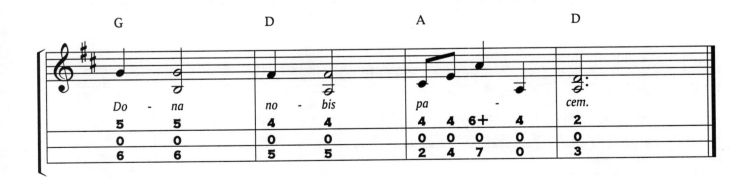

Simple Gifts - DAAA Tuning

Shaker Hymn

The Shakers were a religious group centered in the eastern and midwestern parts of the United States in the 18th and 19th centuries. Among their other teachings, they held beliefs in celibacy and a community holding of goods. This piece refers to the Shakers' expression of faith through copious dancing and singing. "Simple Gifts" is well known outside the Shaker community becasue it was a central musical theme of American composer Aaron Copeland's work, "Appalachian Spring." The song is part of the basic repertoire of most fretted dulcimer players in the United States. I originally arranged "Simple Gifts" in the DAA tuning on the fretted dulcimer to accomodate melody notes below the tonic. This arrangement is for fretted dulcimer with four equidistant strings. If you have a three course dulcimer, ignore the tablature notes for the inside treble string.

Arrangement for Dulcimers © Bonnie Carol 2002

Key of D
Ionian Melody
Tune D A A A
Strummed

♩ = 88

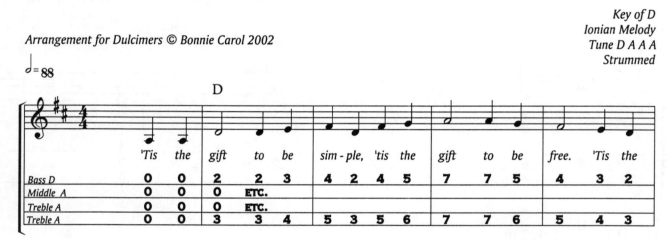

Bonnie@BonnieCarol.com • www.BonnieCarol.com • (303) 258-7763 • 15 Sherwood Road • Nederland, Colorado 80466

Simple Gifts - DADD Tuning

Shaker Hymn

There are so many dulcimer players using the DAD (or DADD) tuning that I include a version of "Simple Gifts" in this tuning. In this arrangement, use a flatpick and pick out the individual notes in the tablature rather than strumming all the strings all the time. Again if you have a three course fretted dulcimer rather than a four, ignore the notes for the inside treble string.

Arrangement for Dulcimers © Bonnie Carol 2002

Key of D
Ionian Melody
Tune D A D D
Strummed

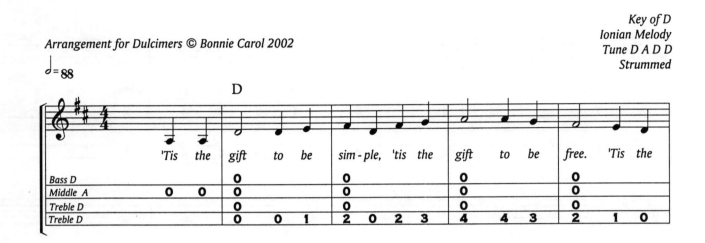

Bonnie@BonnieCarol.com • www.BonnieCarol.com • (303) 258-7763 • 15 Sherwood Road • Nederland, Colorado 80466

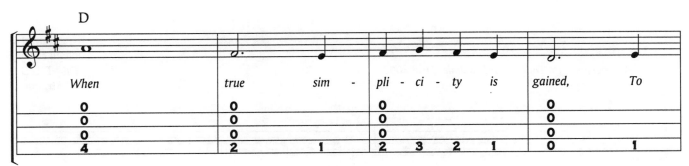

Bonnie@BonnieCarol.com • www.BonnieCarol.com • (303) 258-7763 • 15 Sherwood Road • Nederland, Colorado 80466

Simple Gifts - DGDD Tuning

Shaker Hymn

For some voices, singing "Simple Gifts" in the key of G is easier, so I include a version in that key as well. By looking at all three of these versions of the piece, one can see how to accomodate different tunings and vocal ranges. This arrangement is written for a four-course fretted dulcimer. If you have a three-course one, ignore the notes written for the inside treble string.

Arrangement for Dulcimers © Bonnie Carol 2002

Key of G
Ionian Melody
Tune D G D D
Strummed

Bonnie@BonnieCarol.com • www.BonnieCarol.com • (303) 258-7763 • 15 Sherwood Road • Nederland, Colorado 80466

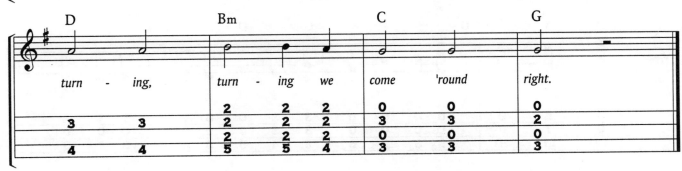

On the Carpenter's Porch – DAA © Princess Harris

The composer of this tune, Princess Harris, is an outstanding hammered dulcimer player and composer from Kansas, and this tune was brought to our dulcimer community by Colorado hammered dulcimer player Tina Gugeler. The tune lays very well on both hammered and fretted dulcimers, and we were initially attracted to it because of the syncopation in the rhythm.

© Princess Harris, 1005 W. 14th, Wichita, KS 67203
(316) 269-4045, Dulcivitae@aol.com; Used by Permission

Arrangement for Fretted Dulcimer by Bonnie Carol

Key of D
Ionian Melody
Tune D A AA
Strummed

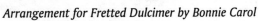

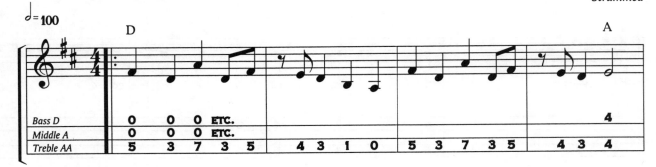

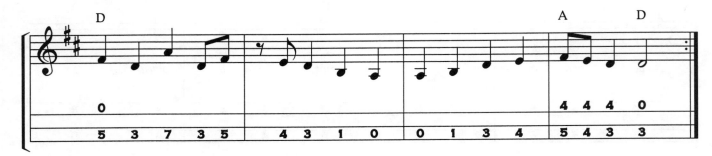

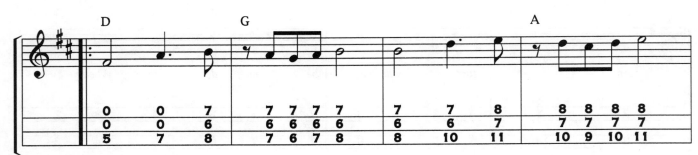

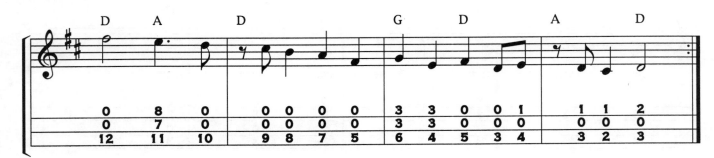

Bonnie@BonnieCarol.com • www.BonnieCarol.com • (303) 258-7763 • 15 Sherwood Road • Nederland, Colorado 80466

On the Carpenter's Porch – DAD   © Princess Harris

This tune lays on the fretted dulcimer well in either the DAA or the DAD tuning. Learning both of these versions is a good way to explore the differences and similarities between these two useful tunings.

© Princess Harris, 1005 W. 14th, Wichita, KS 67203
(316) 269-4045, Dulcivitae@aol.com, Used by Permission

Arrangement for Fretted Dulcimer by Bonnie Carol

Key of D
Ionian Melody
Tune D A DD
Strummed

♩ = 100

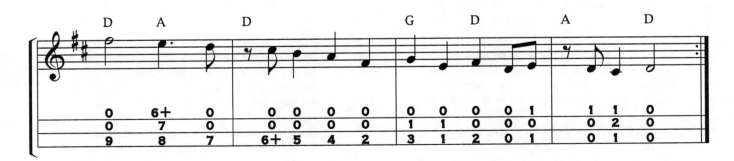

Bonnie@BonnieCarol.com • www.BonnieCarol.com • (303) 258-7763 • 15 Sherwood Road • Nederland, Colorado 80466

Farewell to Tarwathie

Traditional Scottish Song

I learned this song from the singing of Judy Collins on her album, WHALES AND NIGHTENGALES. She sings backed by a chorus of whales. The town of Tarwathie was near Aberdeen, Scotland. The piece was written in the 1850s.

Key of D
Ionian Melody
Tune D A DD
Strummed

Arrangement for Dulcimers © Bonnie Carol 2003

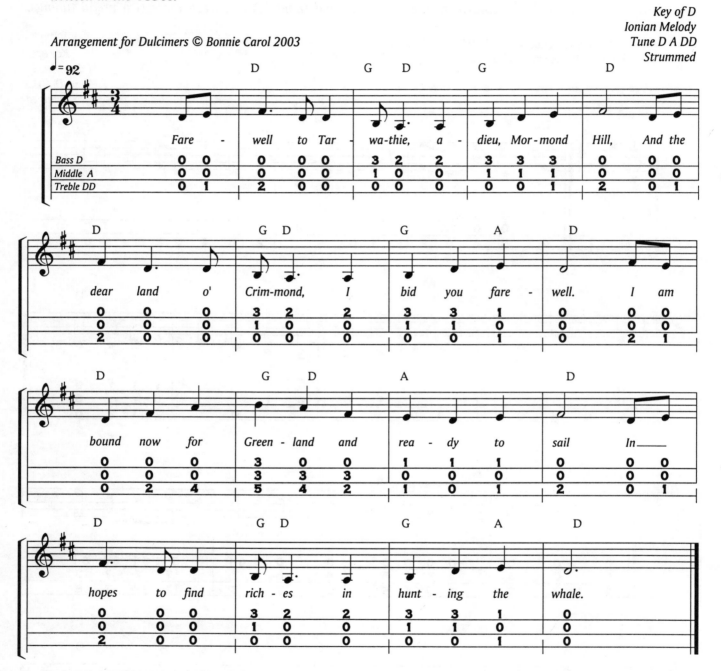

Adieu to my comrades for a while we must part
And likewise the dear lass wha' fair won my heart.
The cold ice of Greenland my love will not chill
And the longer our absence, more loving we'll feel.

Our ship is well-rigged and she's ready to sail.
Our crew they are anxious to follow the whale.
Where the icebergs do float and the stormy winds blow
And the land and the ocean are covered with snow.

Oh the cold coast of Greenland is barren and bare.
No seed-time or harvest is ever known there.
The birds here sing sweetly on mountain and dale,
But there is na' a birdie to sing to the whale.

There is no habitation for a man to live there
And the king of that country is the fierce Greenland bear.
And there'll be no temptation to tarry long there
With our ship bumper full we will homeward repair.

Bonnie@BonnieCarol.com • www.BonnieCarol.com • (303) 258-7763 • 15 Sherwood Road • Nederland, Colorado 80466

Mairi's Wedding

Van Morrison and The Chieftains did a fine vocal rendition of this Scottish wedding march on their album, IRISH HEARTBEAT. The eighth notes are in fact played much more quickly than eights, more like sixteenth or thirty-second notes, giving a much more crisp feel to the tune. On the fretted dulcimer, play only those notes that have tablature numbers.

Arrangement for Dulcimers © Bonnie Carol 2002

Key of G
Ionian Melody
Tune D G DD
Flatpicked

Red Haired Boy

Irish/American Reel

"Red Haired Boy" is a reel of Irish origin found in the United States and in the British Isles under a number of titles. In Ireland it is sung as "Little Beggarman." "Soldier With A Wooden Leg" and "Red Haired Boy" are instrumental versions. Fretted dulcimer pioneer, Richard Fariña, recorded it as "Tommy Makem Fantasy." In the US it is a very common string band piece.

Arrangement for Dulcimers © Bonnie Carol 2001

Key of A
Mixolydian Melody
Tune D A DD, Capo 4
Strummed

Bonnie@BonnieCarol.com • www.BonnieCarol.com • (303) 258-7763 • 15 Sherwood Road • Nederland, Colorado 80466

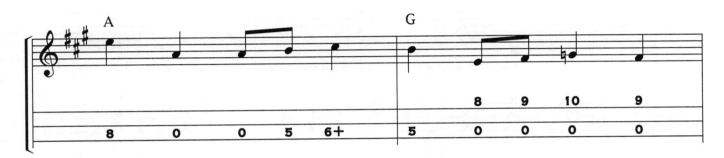

The Little Beggarman Lyrics:

I am a little beggarman a beggin' I have been
For three score and more in this little Isle of Green.
And up to the Liffey and down to Tessague,
And I'm known by the name of the Bold Johnnie Dhu.

CHORUS:
Of all the trades that's goin' sure a beggin' is the best,
For when a man is tired he can sit down have a rest.
He begs for his dinner, he has nothing else to do
Only cut around the corner with his old Ricadoo.

I slept last night in a barn at Currabawn.
A wet night came on and I slipped through the door.
Holes in me shoes and the toes peepin' through
Singin' skiddy-me-re-me-doodlum for old Johnnie Dhu.

I must be gettin' home for it's gettin' late at night.
The fire's all raked and there isn't any light.
And now you've heard me story of the old Ricadoo,
It's good-night and God bless you from old Johnnie Dhu.

Eight More Miles to Louisville

© Grandpa Jones

Colorado dulcimer player Willie Jaeger introduced this song to the local dulcimer community, and it has been a favorite since. It is sometimes played as a singing song, and it has great words. Other times it's played as a square-dance tune.

Words and Music by Louis Marshal Jones, © 1947 by Hill & Range songs, Inc
Copyright Renewed and Assigned to Fort Knox Music Inc. and Trio Music Co.
International Copyright Secured, all Rights Reserved, Used by Permission

Key of D
Ionian Melody
Tune D A DD
Strummed

♩= 100

Verse

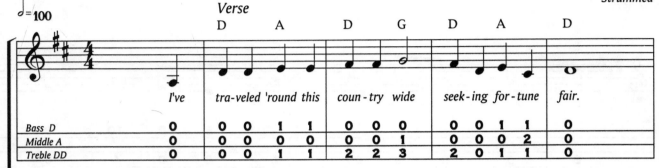

Lyrics: I've tra-veled 'round this coun-try wide seek-ing for-tune fair.

	D	A		D	G	D		A		D
Bass D	0	0	0	1	1	0	0	0	0	1 1	0
Middle A	0	0	0	0	0	0	0	1	0	0 0 2	0
Treble DD	0	0	0	1	1	2	2	3	2	0 1 1	0

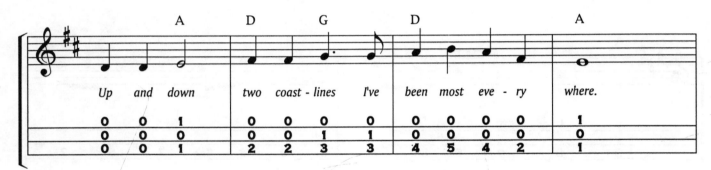

Lyrics: Up and down two coast-lines I've been most eve-ry where.

	A		D	G		D			A
	0	0	1	0	0 0 0	0 0 0 0	1
	0	0	0	0	0 1 1	0 0 0 0	0
	0	0	1	2	2 3 3	4 5 4 2	1

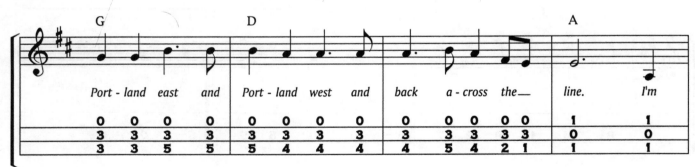

Lyrics: Port-land east and Port-land west and back a-cross the— line. I'm

	G		D				A
	0 0 0 0	0 0 0 0	0 0 0 0	1	1
	3 3 3 3	3 3 3 3	3 3 3 3	0	0
	3 3 5 5	5 4 4 4	4 5 4 2 1	1	1

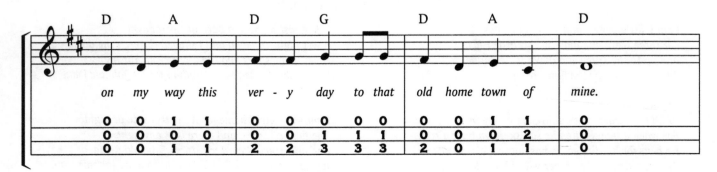

Lyrics: on my way this ver-y day to that old home town of mine.

	D	A		D	G		D	A		D
	0	0	1	1	0 0 0 0	0	0	1	1	0
	0	0	0	0	0 0 1 1	1	0	0	2	0
	0	0	1	1	2 2 3 3	3	2	0 1	1	0

Chorus

Eight more miles and Lou-is-ville will come in-to my view.

Eight more miles and this old world I'll nev-er more be blue. I

knew some day that I'd be back I knew it from the start.

Eight more miles to Lou-is-ville, the home town of my heart.

Everybody's got a gal that he loves best of all.
Mine lives down in Louisville, she's long and she is tall.
She's not the kind that you can find ramblin' round this land.
I'm on my way this very day to seek her heart and hand.

Now I can picture in my mind the place we'll call our home.
A humble little cabin where we never more will roam.
The place that's right for this love sight is in them bluegrass hills,
Where gently flows the Ohio in a place called Louisville.

Bonnie@BonnieCarol.com • www.BonnieCarol.com • (303) 258-7763 • 15 Sherwood Road • Nederland, CO 80466

Golden Slippers - Duet

by James Bland

Black composer James A. Bland was a minstrel show songwriter of the 1800's. The tune is always a favorite of the hammered dulcimer players and can frequently be heard at squaredances. It lends itself magnificently to harmony, so I have written a duet harmony part in smaller notes.

Arrangement © Bonnie Carol 1997

Key of G
Ionian Melody
Tune D G DD
Strummed

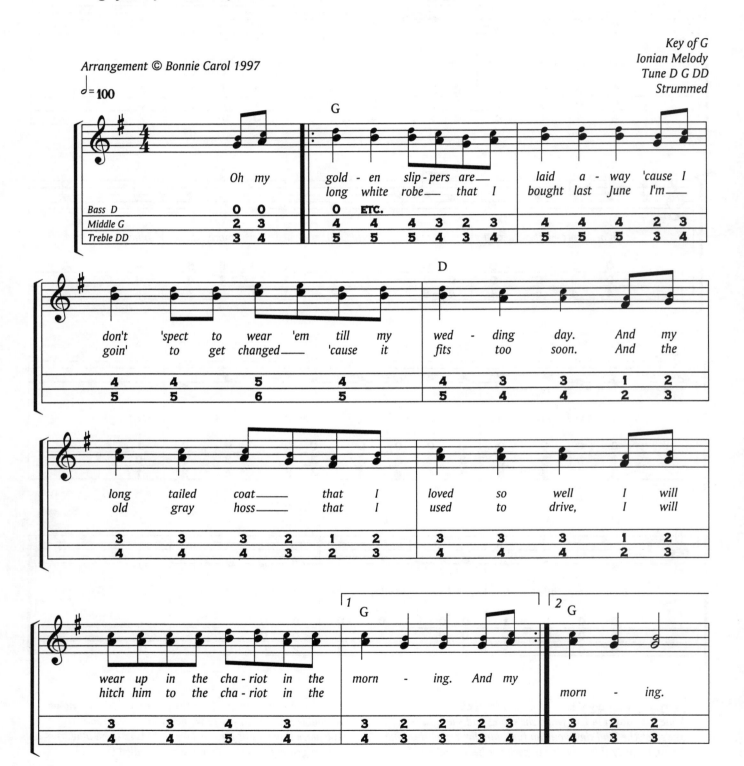

Oh, my old banjo hangs on the wall
'Cause it ain't been tuned since way last fall.
But the darkies all say we will have a good time
When we ride up in the chariot in the morning.

There's old brother Ben and Sister Luce;
They will telegraph the news to Uncle Bacco Juice.
What great camp meetin' there will be that day
When we ride up in the chariot in the morning.

So, it's good bye children, I will have to go
Where the rain don't fall and the wind don't blow.
And your ulster coats, why you will not need
When you ride up in the chariot in the morning.

But your GOLDEN SLIPPERS must be nice and clean;
And your age must be just sweet sixteen.
And your white kid gloves you will have to wear
When you ride up in the chariot in the morning.

Bonnie@BonnieCarol.com • www.BonnieCarol.com • (303) 258-7763 • 15 Sherwood Road • Nederland, Colorado 80466

Oh, My Little Darlin'

Appalachian Fiddle Tune

I learned "Oh, My Little Darlin' " from Lois Hornbostel during one of those all-day jam sessions touring musicians engage in during days off. It was originally collected by the Library of Congress from a banjo player named Thaddeus Willingham of Gulfport, Mississippi, thus qualifying it for official Southern tune status. I liked the tune but always felt it needed more lyrics, so I wrote a whole story one day as I drove through Navajo Country in the great Southwest. The feel of the tune is very typical of southern Appalachian fiddle music which sports a highly emphasized off beat called a "shuffle": the second and fourth beats of the measures are emphasized over the first and third. I noted these accents in the hammered dulcimer notation.

Arrangement for Fretted Dulcimer by Lois Hornbostel
Arrangement for Hammered Dulcimer by Bonnie Carol

Key of D
Tune D A DD
Mixolydian Melody
Strummed

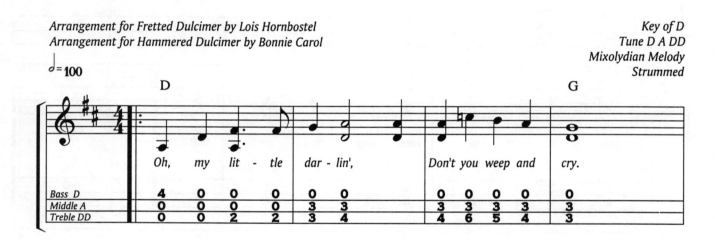

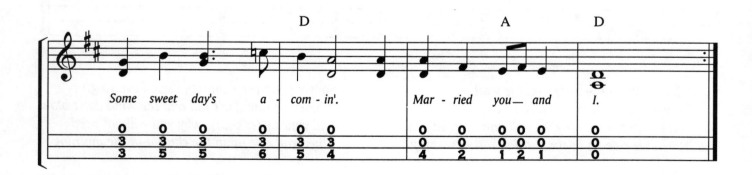

Bonnie@BonnieCarol.com • www.BonnieCarol.com • (303) 258-7763 • 15 Sherwood Road • Nederland, CO 80466

Sarah sows the cornfield
Plows the valley brown.
Sarah picks the cotton.
Drive those bales to town. *

Up and down the railroad
Cross that county line.
Banjo on my shoulder,
Gonna see that man of mine. +

Jimmy came a-courtin'.
Sarah baked a pie.
He saw the twinkle in her eye.
Married in the rye. *

O My Little Darlin',
Don't you weep and cry.
Some sweet day's a comin'
Married you and I. +

Jimmy drives a wagon.
Jimmy holds the line.
Kill yourself a-laughin'.
See them horses flyin'. +

Little Janey Tucker,
Born on grandad's farm.
Grew up herdin' cattle.
Lasso on her arm. *

Janey grey up hearty.
Mom's twinkle in her eye.
Cherokee man from the railroad town
Wants her by his side. *

O My Little Darlin',
Don't you weep and moan.
Some sweet days a-comin'
Gonna take my baby home. +

+ *Traditional verses*
*Verses composed by Bonnie Carol

Bonnie@BonnieCarol.com • www.BonnieCarol.com • (303) 258-7763 • 15 Sherwood Road • Nederland, CO 80466

Greensleeves ~ EBD Tuning

English Air

"Greensleeves" is not a strictly modal song. The melody uses both the Aeolian and Dorian modes, and it has a couple of notes that are outside either mode. Players of diatonic instruments such as the dulcimers, whistle, or button accordion alter the melody in various ways to accomodate the extra-modal melody and chords. There are pinches and drags in the fretted dulcimer tablature. You can learn how to do these in DUST OFF THAT DULCIMER AND DANCE: A MOUNTAIN DULCIMER INSTRUCTION BOOK.

Key of Em
Dorian and Aeolian Melody
Tune E B DD
Fingerpicked

Arrangement for dulcimers © Bonnie Carol, 2002

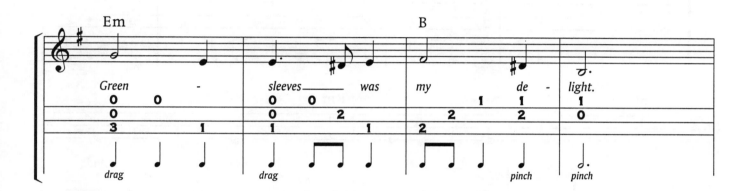

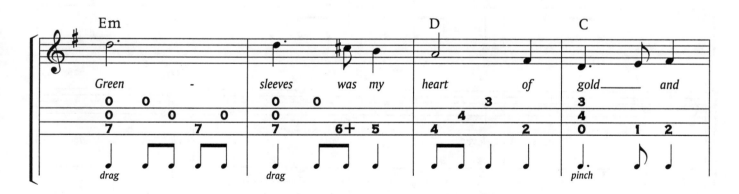

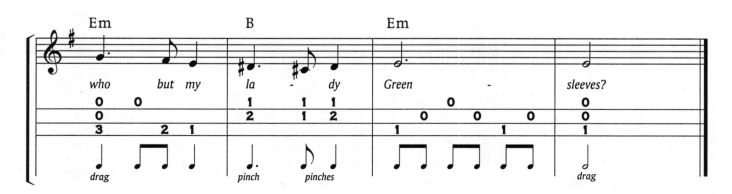

Bonnie@BonnieCarol.com • www.BonnieCarol.com • (303) 258-7763 • 15 Sherwood Road • Nederland, Colorado 80466

Greensleeves ~ DAD Tuning

A good tour through various tunings and modes and how to use them in arranging a piece can be achieved by learning these three versions of "Greensleeves." For the hammered dulcimer, add one or two chord notes whenever the chords change for a complete solo arrangement.

Arrangement for dulcimers © Bonnie Carol, 2002

Key of Em
Aeolian and Dorian Melody
Tune D A DD
Fingerpicked

Greensleeves ~ DAD, Capo 1 Tuning

This version of "Greensleeves" has the same melody and chord structure as the DAD version has, but it is accomplished by using a capo instead of fretting to the chords. Comparing the two will give you more ideas about various ways to arrange a tune.

Key of Em
Dorian and Aeolian Melody
Tune D A DD, Capo 1
Fingerpicked

Arrangement for dulcimers © Bonnie Carol, 2002

Bonnie@BonnieCarol.com • www.BonnieCarol.com • (303) 258-7763 • 15 Sherwood Road • Nederland, Colorado 80466

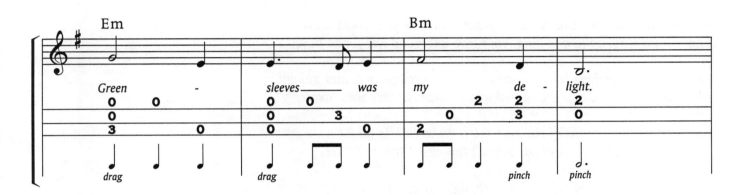

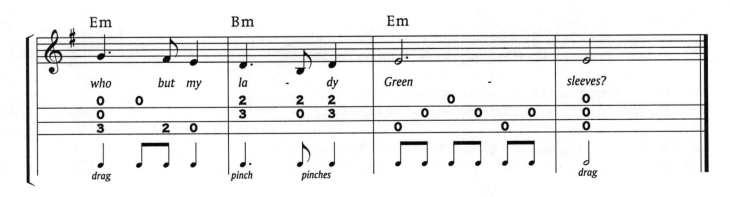

Greensleeves and What Child Is This Lyrics

"Greensleeves" is an English air and song from Shakespeare's era. The Christmas hymn "What Child Is This?" borrowed the melody.

GREENSLEEVES

Alas, my Love, you do me wrong to cast me off discourteously.
And I have loved you so long, delighting in your company.

CHORUS:
> *Greensleeves was all my joy. Greensleeves was my delight.*
> *Greensleeves was my heart of gold and who but my lady Greensleeves?*

I have been ready at your hand to grant whatever you would crave.
I have both waged life and land, your love and good will for to have.

I bought thee kerchers to thy head that were wrought fine and gallantly.
I kept these both at board and bed which cost my purse well favoredly.

I bought thee petticoats of the best the cloth so fine as might be.
I gave thee jewels for thy chest, and all this cost I spent on thee.

Will I will pray to God on high that though my constancy mayst see,
And that yet once before I die, though will vouch safe to love me.

Greensleeves, now farewell! Adieu! God I pray to prosper thee!
For I am still thy lover true, come once again and love me.

WHAT CHILD IS THIS?

What child is this, who, laid to rest, on Mary's lap is sleeping?
Whom angels greet with anthems sweet, while shepherds watch are keeping?

CHORUS:
> *This, this is Christ the King, whom shepherds guard and angels sing.*
> *Haste, haste to bring Him laud, The Babe, the Son of Mary!*

Why liest He in such mean estate where ox and ass are feeding?
Good Christian, fear for sinners here the silent Word is pleading.

So bring Him incense, gold, and myrrh, come peasant king to own Him.
The King of kings, salvation brings, let loving hearts enthrone Him.

The Wee Reel

Our Boulder, Colorado, dulcimer group has been blessed to have composer and guitar player Billy Ikler among us. He composed this tune, and it has been a favorite of the hammered and fretted dulcimer players, as well as the whistle and guitar players since.

© Billy Ikler, POB 873, Nederland, CO 80466
(303) 258-3858, ktbi@indra.com, Used by Permission
Arrangement for Dulcimers by Bonnie Carol

Key of E minor
Aeolian Melody
Tune D A DD, Capo 1st Fret
Flatpicked

Capo 1

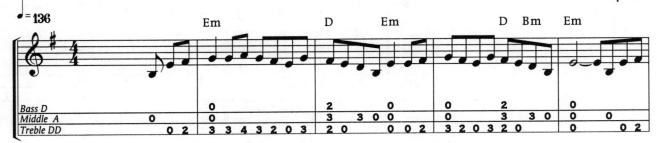

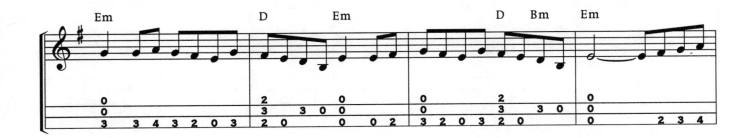

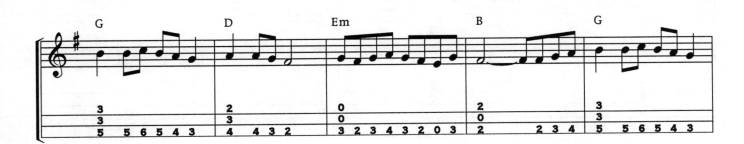

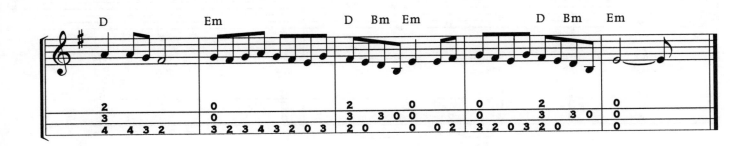

The Parting Glass

Traditional Irish Song

On the fretted dulcimer, play only notes where there are tablature numbers. Use an assortment of pinches and drags to get the individual notes. I learned this from the singing of Michael Hubbert on the PACIFIC RIM DULCIMER PROJECT recording. We've ended many a fine evening of music with it.

Key of Bm
Aeolian Melody
Tune D A DD
Fingerpicked

If I had money enough to spend, and leisure time to sit awhile,
There is a fair maid in this town, that sorely has my heart beguiled.
Her rosy cheeks and ruby lips, I own, she has my heart in thrall.
Then fill to me The Parting Glass, good night and joy be with you all.

Bonnie@BonnieCarol.com • www.BonnieCarol.com • (303) 258-7763 • 15 Sherwood Road • Nederland, Colorado 80466

Sí Beag, Sí Mór

Celtic Harp Tune by Turlough O'Carolan

Sí are fairies, or immortal beings, who are central characters in the mythology of Ireland. The song title, "Sí Beag, Sí Mór," meaning "Little Fairy Hill, Big Fairy Hill," follows a myth concerning an altercation between two Sí who lived under the hills. For the fretted dulcimer, it is intended that you fingerpick only those notes where there is a tablature number. As usual, where there are several notes being played at once, use a pinch or a drag. On the hammered dulcimer, note the rolling chord, or arpeggio symbols. Begin with the lowest note and go quickly to the highest.

Arrangement for Dulcimers © Bonnie Carol, 1996

Key of D
Tune D A DD
Ionian Mode
Fingerpicked

Bonnie@BonnieCarol.com • www.BonnieCarol.com • (303) 258-7763 • 15 Sherwood Road • Nederland, CO 80466

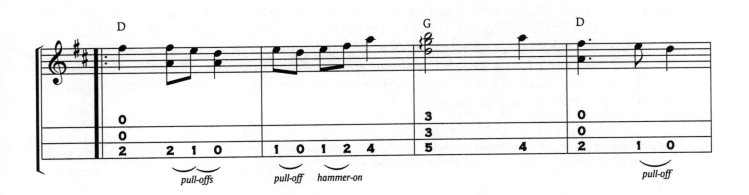

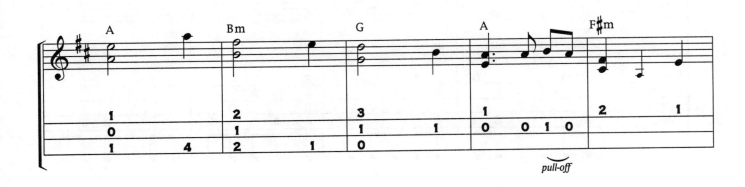

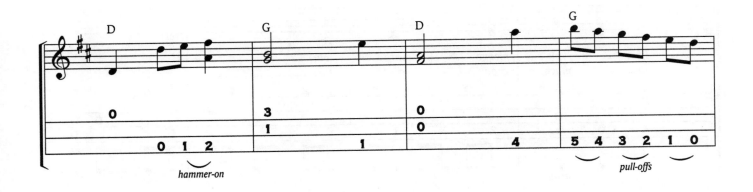

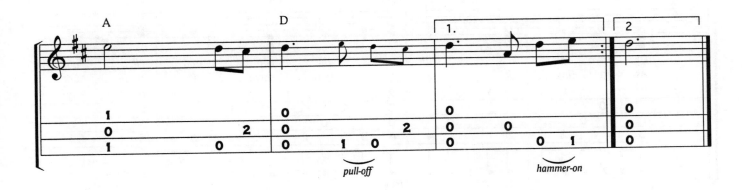

Drink To Me Only

Words by Ben Johnson (1573 – 1637)

You can hear Howie Mitchell himself playing this arrangement of "Drink To Me Only" on his album, THE MOUNTAIN DULCIMER: HOW TO MAKE IT AND PLAY IT (AFTER A FASHION) *available from Folk Legacy Records, Inc., Sharon, Connecticut, 06069, folklegacy@snet.net, www.folklegacy.com. The piece is also called "To Celia." I have included numerous notations for fingerpicking flourishes (hammer-ons, pull-off, drags, and slides). The hammered dulcimer arrangement has many three-note chords. Play the lowest note first and end with the melody note.*

Key of D
Tune D A D D
Ionian Mode
Fingerpicked

Fretted Dulcimer Arrangement by Howie Mitchell
Hammered Dulcimer Arrangement and Transcription by Bonnie Carol

Dolores Waltz

© Billy Ikler 2000

My neighbor and frequent music partner, Billy Ikler, is a stellar composer, and when he composed Dolores Waltz and brought it to our dulcimer group, it was a hit. In Spanish, the word "dolor" means pain, and it has the same root as the name "Dolores." Although he wrote it on guitar, it lays quite well on both dulcimers. On the fretted dulcimer, whether you fingerpick or flatpick, play only the notes which have tablature numbers. Use an assortment of drags and pinches to play the chords. In the hammered dulcimer music, the small notes are filler notes, not part of the melody.

© Billy Ikler, POB 873, Nederland, CO 80466
(303) 258-3858, ktbi@indra.com, Used by Permission

Key of Bm
Aeolian Mode
Tune D A D D
Fingerpicked or Flatpicked

Arrangement for Dulcimers by Bonnie Carol

Bonnie@BonnieCarol.com • www.BonnieCarol.com • (303) 258-7763 • 15 Sherwood Road • Nederland, Colorado 80466

The Road to Lisdoonvarna

Traditional Irish Jig

When I visited Ireland, I drove the road to Lisdoonvarna, and it is certainly worthy of a namesake song with its many switchbacks falling gracefully down a long mountainside. On the fretted dulcimer, I strum IN out in, IN out in for the 1 2 3, 4 5 6 beats. This strum pattern automatically sets up the jig feel with accents on the first and fourth beats.

Key of Em
Aeolian Melody
Tune D A DD, Capo 1
Strummed

Arrangement for Dulcimers © Bonnie Carol 2001

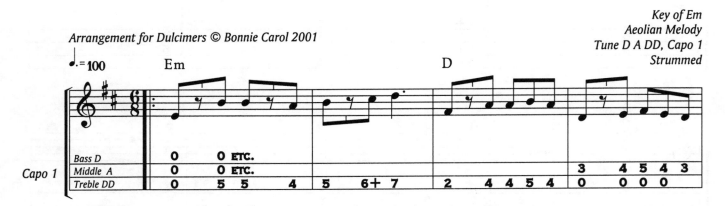

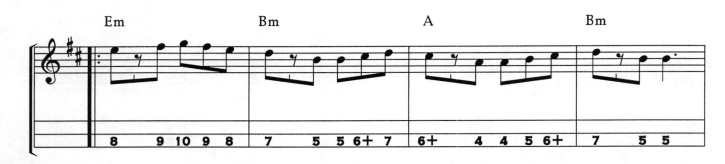

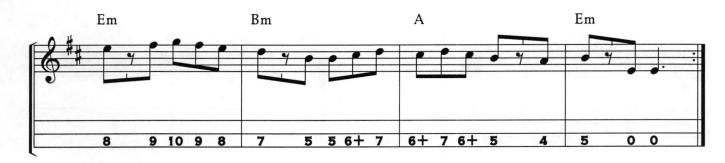

Far Away

There are many long chords in the hammered dulcimer music. Begin with the lowest note and play to the highest. In the fretted dulcimer tablature, flatpick notes which have tab numbers but not others.

© Pete Jung, 15 Rossman Ave., Hudson, NY 12534
(518) 828-9917, prj@mhcable.com, Used by Permission
Arrangement for dulcimers by Cathy Kerry and Bonnie Carol

Key of D
Ionian Melody
Tune D A AA
Flatpicked

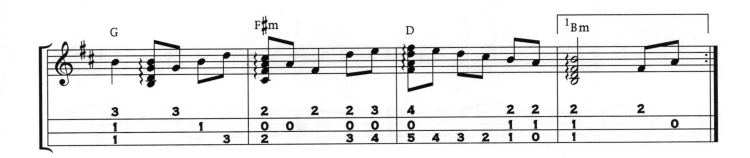

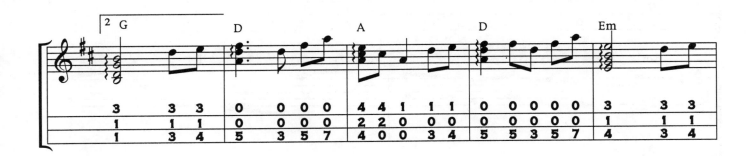

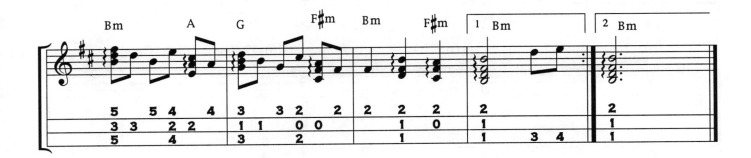

King of the Fairies

Traditional Irish Set Dance

The chord progression arranged by Mike Connolly and Marc Painter as well as the syncopation of the melody gives this arrangement a decidedly jazzy feel. Many of the jazz chords are not available on either dulcimer, so I have a couple of suggestions. If a hammered dulcimer and guitar are playing the piece, the hammered dulcimer should play only melody and leave the chords to the guitar. If a fretted dulcimer and guitar are playing, the fretted dulcimer can flatpick only the melody notes, or the guitar can omit the optional chords, enclosed in parentheses. Ah yes, there are many ways to interpret a piece of music - there are at least three on this page!

Guitar Accompaniment by Marc Painter and Mike Connolly
Arrangement for Dulcimers © Bonnie Carol 1995

Key of E Minor
Aeolian Melody
Tune D A DD, Capo 1
Flatpicked

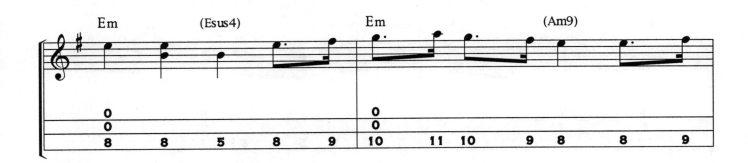

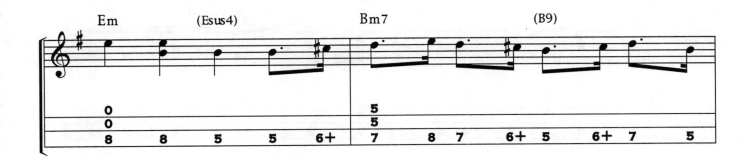

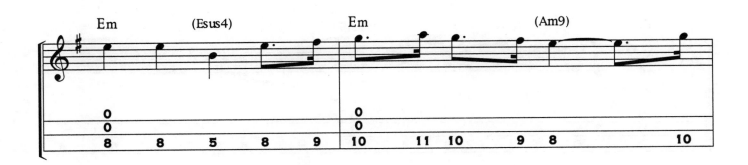

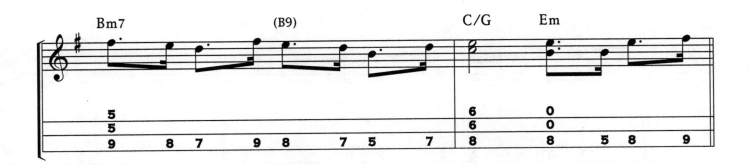

Bonnie@BonnieCarol.com • www.BonnieCarol.com • (303) 258-7763 • 15 Sherwood Road • Nederland, Colorado 80466

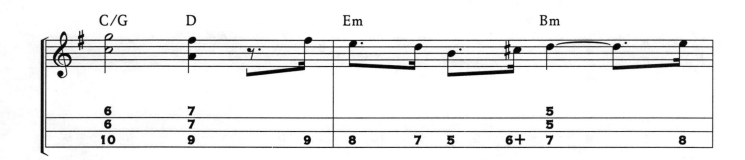

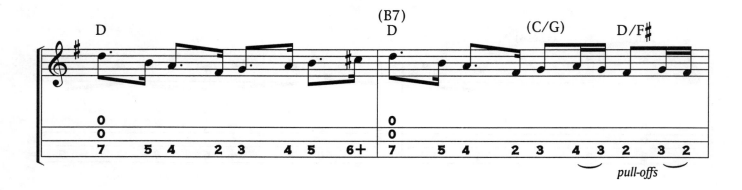

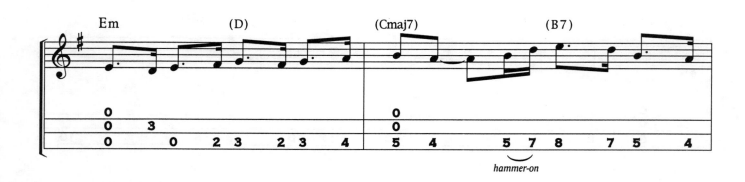

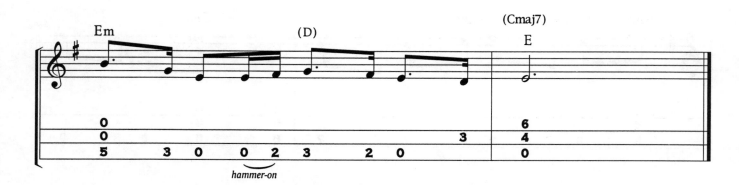

Bonnie@BonnieCarol.com • www.BonnieCarol.com • (303) 258-7763 • 15 Sherwood Road • Nederland, Colorado 80466

The Irish Washerwoman

Irish Jig

*It seems to me that people can listen to a whole evening of Irish music and not until a jig is played do they say, "Ah, you are playing IRISH music." Somehow the jig defines Irish music for many people, and this is probably the most well-known Irish jig. I sometimes take the liberty of updating the politics by calling the piece "Irish Washerperson." A jig is counted **1** 2 3 **4** 5 6, with accents on the **first** and **fourth** beats. This particular jig has no rhythmic breaks in the melody and so cries out for accents to give interest and variety in the rhythm. On the hammered dulcimer, alternate hammers with each note, **LEFT** right left, **RIGHT** left right, and the accents will fall in a different hand with each group of three. On the fretted dulcimer, I strum **IN** out in, **IN** out in for the **1** 2 3, **4** 5 6 beats. This strum pattern automatically sets up the jig feel with accents on the first and fourth beats. Strum all the strings throughout, but only change your fret position when there is a new tablature number.*

Key of G
Ionian Melody
Tune D G DD
Strummed

Arrangement for Dulcimers © Bonnie Carol 2001

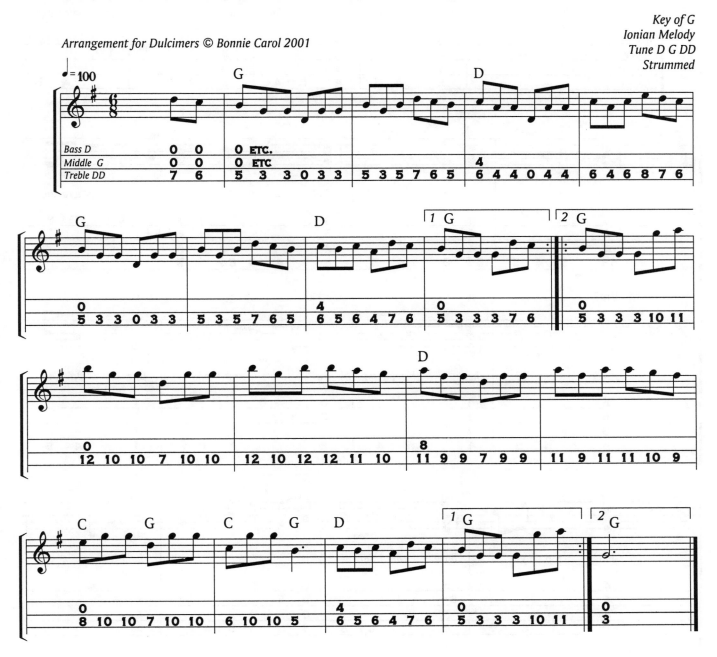

Dark Island

Music by Iain Maclachlan, Words by David Silver

The "dark island" is one of the Hebrides Islands off the coast of Scotland. If you have a three-course rather than a four-course fretted dulcimer, simply ignore the tablature numbers for the inner treble string. Play only notes with tablature numbers, and use a drag for the multi-note chords.

Key of A
Ionian Melody
Tune D A D D
Fingerpicked

Arrangement for Dulcimers by Bonnie Carol and Tina Adcock 2001

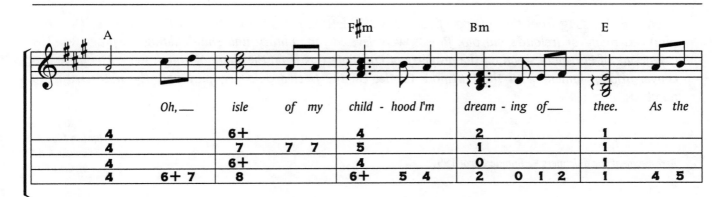

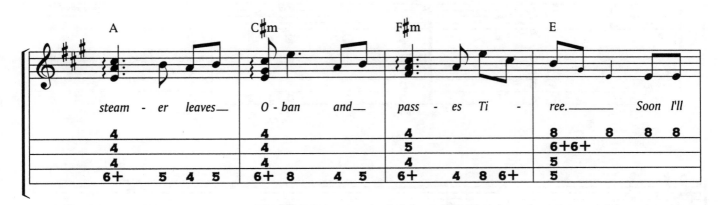

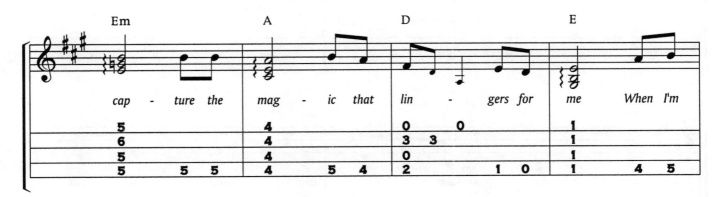

Bonnie@BonnieCarol.com • www.BonnieCarol.com • (303) 258-7763 • 15 Sherwood Road • Nederland, Colorado 80466

Bonny Portmore

Irish Traditional Song

I learned this song from the singing of Lorena McKinnett on her album, THE VISIT. She writes, "Over the centuries many of Ireland's old oak forests were leveled for military and ship-building purposes. . . The Great Oak of Portmore stood on the property of Portmore Castle on the shore of Lough Beg." The piece is a conversational lament with the Portmore Castle. On the fretted dulcimer, play only the notes with tab numbers.

Key of D
Ionian Melody
Tune D A AA
Fingerpicked

Arrangement for dulcimers © Bonnie Carol 1997

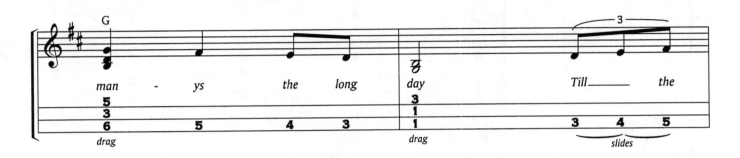

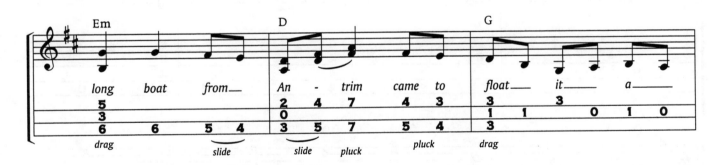

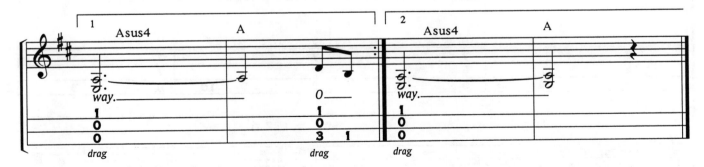

O Bonny Portmore, you shine where you stand
And the more I think on you the more I think long.
If I had you now as I had once before
All the lords in Old England would not purchase Portmore.

All the birds in the forest they bitterly weep
Saying, "Where shall we shelter or where shall we sleep?"
For the oak and the ash they are all cutten down
And the walls of Bonny Portmore are all down to the ground.

Bonnie@BonnieCarol.com • www.BonnieCarol.com • (303) 258-7763 • 15 Sherwood Road • Nederland, Colorado 80466

Westphalia Waltz

I've always thought the most interesting thing about this piece is the chord progression, and it was not until fretted dulcimer wizard Steve Seifert set me on the right path relative to tuning, that I could find all these unusual chords on the fretted dulcimer. The piece can frequently be heard in the Texas style fiddle contests. On the fretted dulcimer, strum across all the strings throughout, but change finger positions whenever a new tablature number appears. In other words, maintain each chord position until a new one appears.

Key of G
Ionian Melody
Tune D A D D, capo 3
Strummed

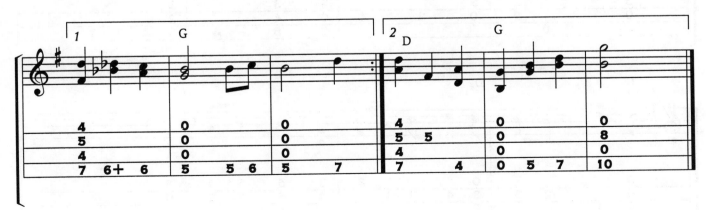

Tommy Bhetty's Waltz

Celtic Waltz

Lower Fretted Dulcimer Version

This waltz was very popular among the participants in our Colorado dulcimer community, and we arranged it several different ways. Here is a version in which the fretted dulcimer part is played in a low register. Play only those notes which have tablature numbers. I make suggestions about pinches and drags in the first line but then leave it to you to determine exactly how to execute the fingerpicking for the rest of the piece. I learned this waltz from a favorite student, John Putnam, and he learned it from the playing of the Celtic group, Altan, from their album, THE FIRST TEN YEARS.

Key of G
Ionian Mode
Tune D G DD
Fingerpicked

Arrangement © Bonnie Carol 1997

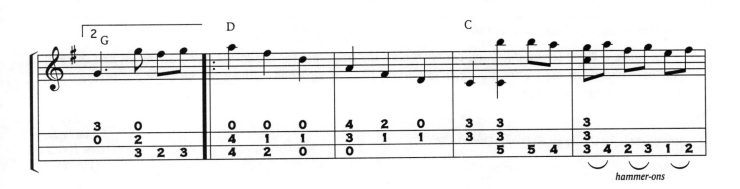

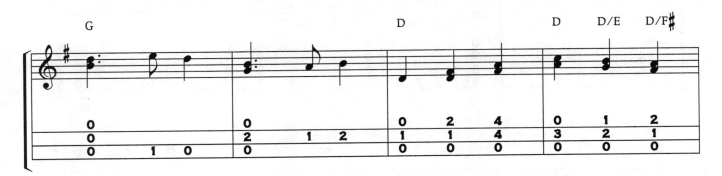

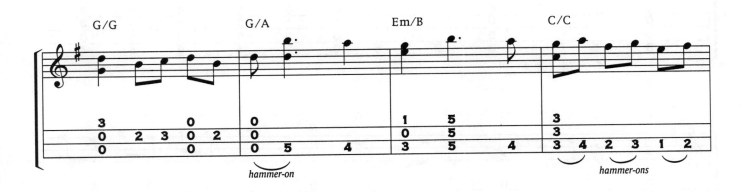

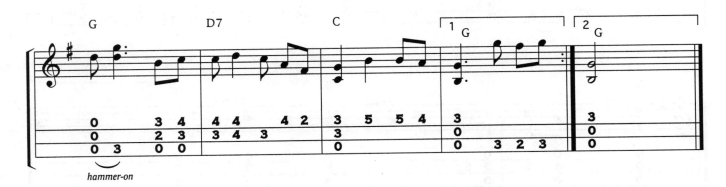

Tommy Bhetty's Waltz

Celtic Waltz

Higher Fretted Dulcimer Version

If you have a three string dulcimer, simply ignore the tablature for the inside treble string. When there are full note chords in the fretted dulcimer tablature, use a drag: that is, drag the index finger across all the strings from bass to treble.

Key of G
Ionian Melody
Tune D G D D
Fingerpicked

Arrangement for Dulcimers © Bonnie Carol 1997

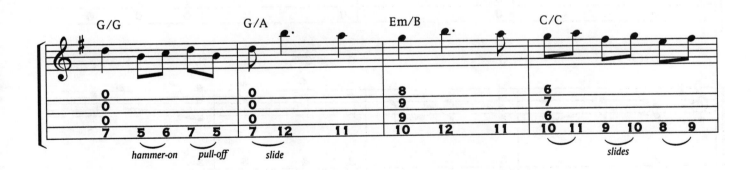

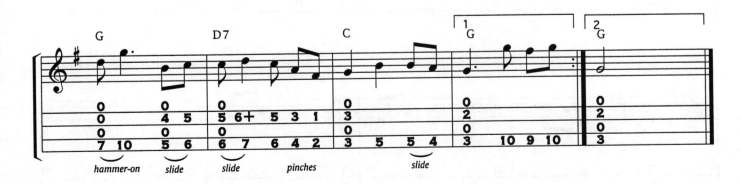

Tommy Bhetty's Waltz

Celtic Waltz

Accompaniment

In this version of "Tommy Bhetty's Waltz," the fretted dulcimer plays a chordal accompaniment. One of the most interesting things about this piece is the chord progression. On the Altan recording, THE FIRST TEN YEARS, *the guitar plays an accompaniment something like the fretted dulcimer part notated here.*

Key of G
Ionian Mode
Tune D G DD
Strummed

Arrangement for Dulcimers © Bonnie Carol 1997

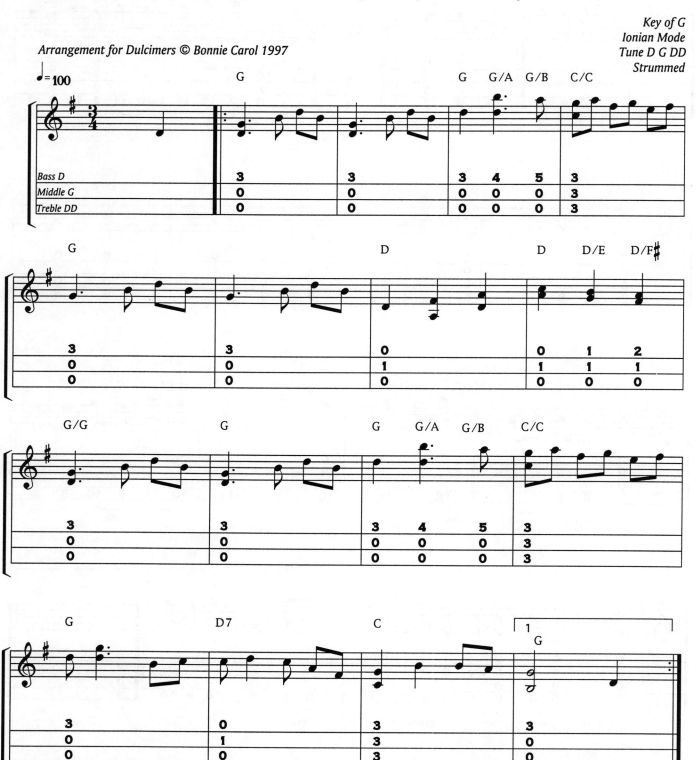

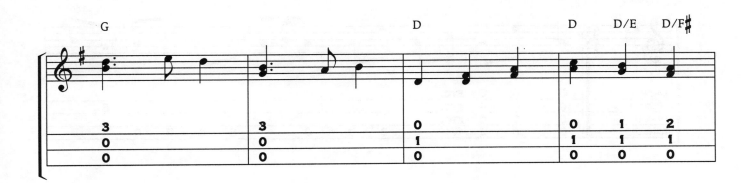

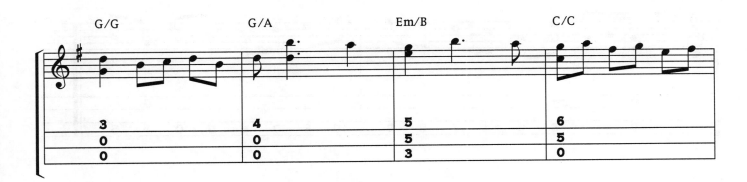

Bonnie@BonnieCarol.com • www.BonnieCarol.com • (303) 258-7763 • 15 Sherwood Road • Nederland, Colorado 80466

Gravel Walks

Traditional Irish Reel

This is a very dynamic tune, beginning in A major for the A part, then to A minor for the B and C parts, and then in the D part, the key of C major. In the fretted dulcimer arrangement, you should strum the piece throughout. Once a chord or finger position is noted in the fretted dulcimer tablature, keep this position until another tablature number appears. On the hammered dulcimer, play the 16th notes by bouncing one hammer from the first sixteenth note to the second, rather than hammering each 16th note individually.

Arrangement for Dulcimers © Bonnie Carol 2001

Keys of A, Am & C
Mixolydian & Dorian Melody
Tune D A D D, capo 4
Strummed

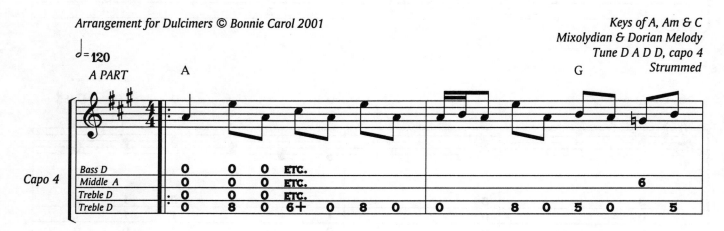

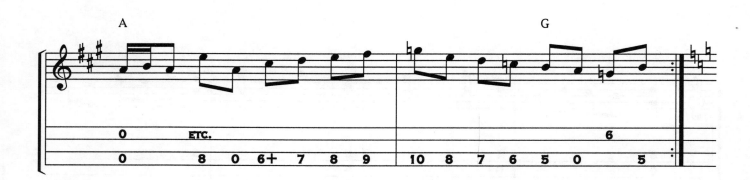

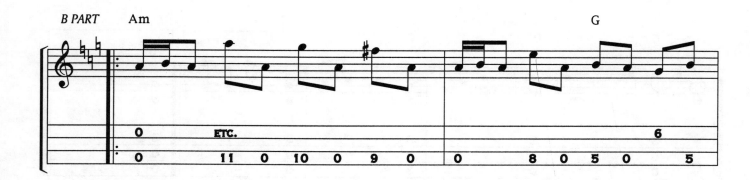

Bonnie@BonnieCarol.com • www.BonnieCarol.com • (303) 258-7763 • 15 Sherwood Road • Nederland, Colorado 80466

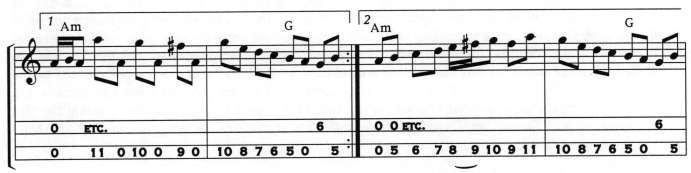

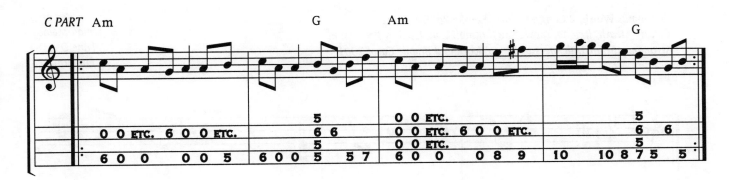

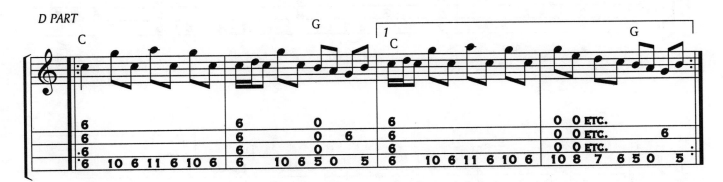

Inís Oírr

Inís Oírr is the smallest of the Aran Islands off the west coast of Ireland near Galway, and this tune bearing the same name is one of my favorite Celtic airs. The composer, Thomas Walsh, lives near Dublin and plays button accordion in the regular sessions in Dublin's Temple Bar. He wrote the tune while visiting the island of Inís Oír in the seventies. I have seen the name spelled "Inishere," "Inisheer," and "Inís Oírr," in Irish, as spelled here. The tune itself has been passed around the United States via the oral tradition, and by the time it got to Colorado where I live, it had a different chord progression and some variations in the rhythmic interpretation from what Thomas Walsh plays. That is what I have transcribed here. On the next page you can find Thomas Walsh's own version. On the fretted dulcimer, use drags and pinches to execute the multi-note chords.

© Thomas Walsh, 2 Congress Park, Rooske Rd. Dunboyne
County Meath, Ireland, tppwalsh@hotmail.com, Used by Permission
Arrangement for Dulcimers by Tina Adcock and Bonnie Carol 2001

Key of G
Ionian Melody
Tune D A DD
Fingerpicked

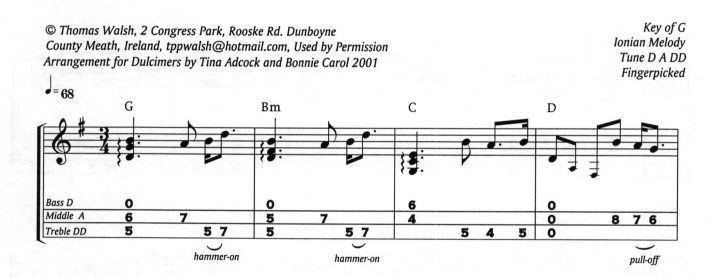

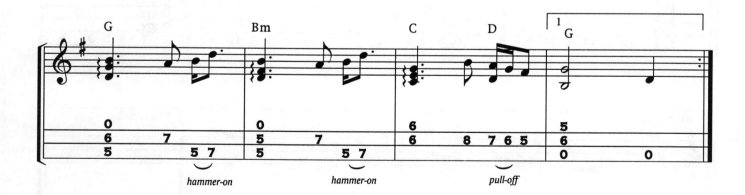

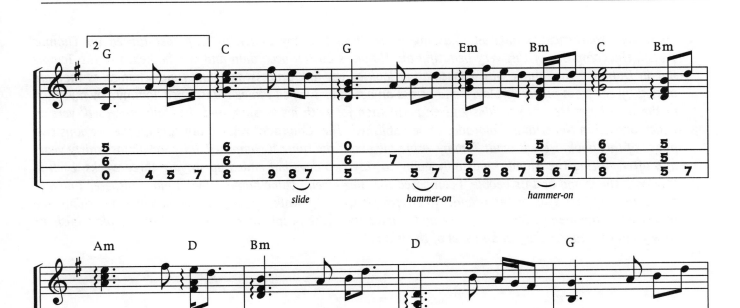

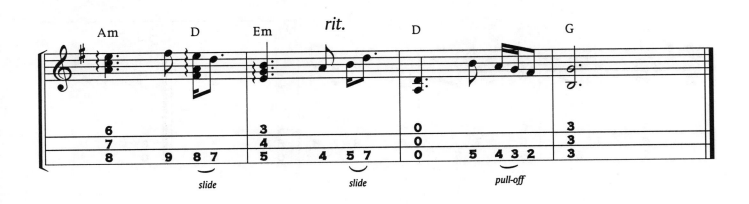

Bonnie@BonnieCarol.com • www.BonnieCarol.com • (303) 258-7763 • 15 Sherwood Road • Nederland, Colorado 80466

Inishere

Some very sophisticated internet sleuthing by my friend, Penny Bauer, at long last turned up Thomas Walsh, the composer of this very beautiful air. He plays button accordion and can be heard in the Temple Bar in Dublin. I thought it was a fascinating look at the folk process and how tunes change as they are passed by ear from player to player and across an ocean or two, so I have transcribed Tommy's own version of the tune here. He has graciously given permission for both his version, and the "folk processed" version which arrived in Nederland, Colorado, to be published. The "Colorado" version appears on the previous two pages of this book. Here is what Tommy wrote me about the tune: "I composed 'Inishere' almost thirty years ago after visiting the island. I was only going to stay two days but ended up staying three weeks. I fell in love with the island and its people. I composed the tune when I came home. When I play 'Inishere,' I always remember my first visit to the island. No electricity, the long walks, going out in the currachs, riding the waves while the men rowed. The peace and tranquility of the people and the island. I like to play 'Inishere' slowly in order to get the feel and soul of the island."

Arrangement for Dulcimers by Bonnie Carol 2001

Key of G
Ionian Melody
Tune D A DD
Fingerpicked

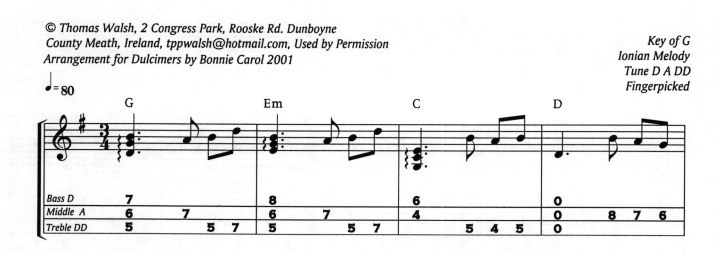

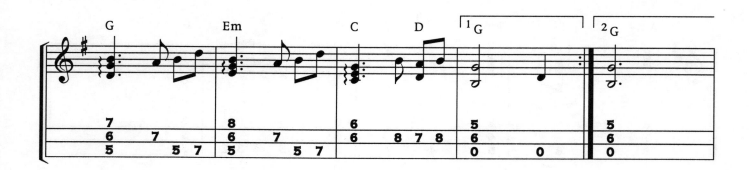

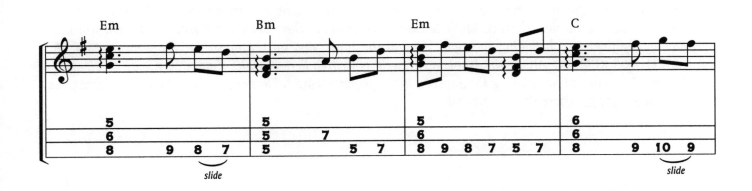

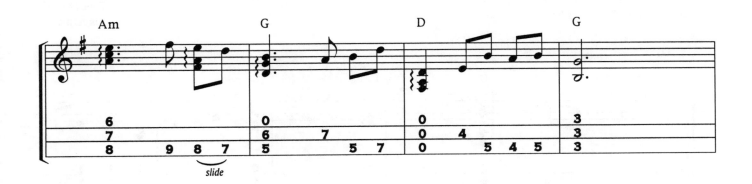

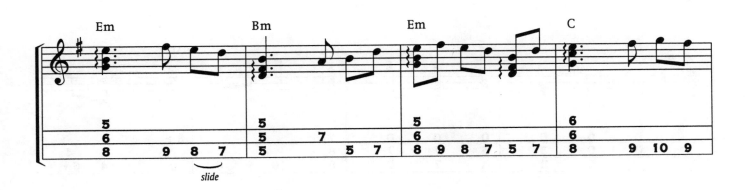

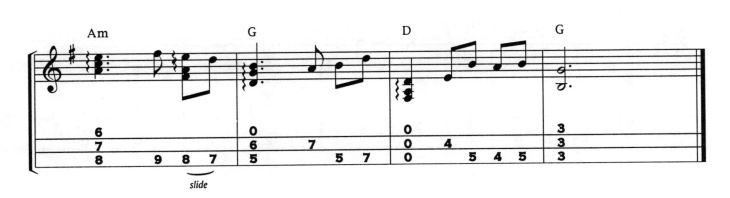

Bonnie@BonnieCarol.com • www.BonnieCarol.com • (303) 258-7763 • 15 Sherwood Road • Nederland, Colorado 80466

Ashokan Farewell

by Jay Ungar

This is the beautiful air written by Jay Ungar and used in Ken Burns' television series THE CIVIL WAR. Jay and his wife and musical partner, Molly Mason, have written other tunes in the traditional vein which are among my favorites, including the tune "Around the Horn" and all the music for the documentary film, BROTHER'S KEEPER. Although "Ashokan Farewell" is written here in waltz time, I play it as an air with a free rhythm, unless I am playing for dancers. In the fingerpicking tablature for the mountain dulcimer, play only those strings where there is a number.

Key of D
Ionian Mode
Tune D A DD
Fingerpicked

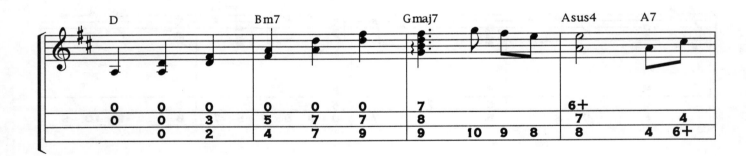

Bonnie@BonnieCarol.com • www.BonieCarol.com • (303) 258-7763 • 15 Sherwood Road • Nederland, CO 80466

Miss Rowan Davies

© Phil Cunningham

Accordion player and composer Phil Cunningham is one of the most gifted of the contemporary Scottish musicians. He's a veteran of the Scottish group Silly Wizard and currently tours with fiddler Aly Bain. This tune can be heard on his recording AIRS AND GRACES. To use this arrangement for a three course dulcimer simply ignore the tablature for the inner treble string. With this approach you may also want to move an occasional inner treble string note to the other treble string. Again, use a combination of drags and pinches to execute the multi-note chords.

©Phil Cunningham, Cunningham Audio Productions, Ltd, Crask of Aigas, By Beauly
Inverness-shire, Scotland, IV4 7AD, capdonna@cali.co.uk, Used by Permission
Arrangement for Dulcimers © Bonnie Carol 2000

Key of G
Ionian Melody
Tune D G D D
Fingerpicked

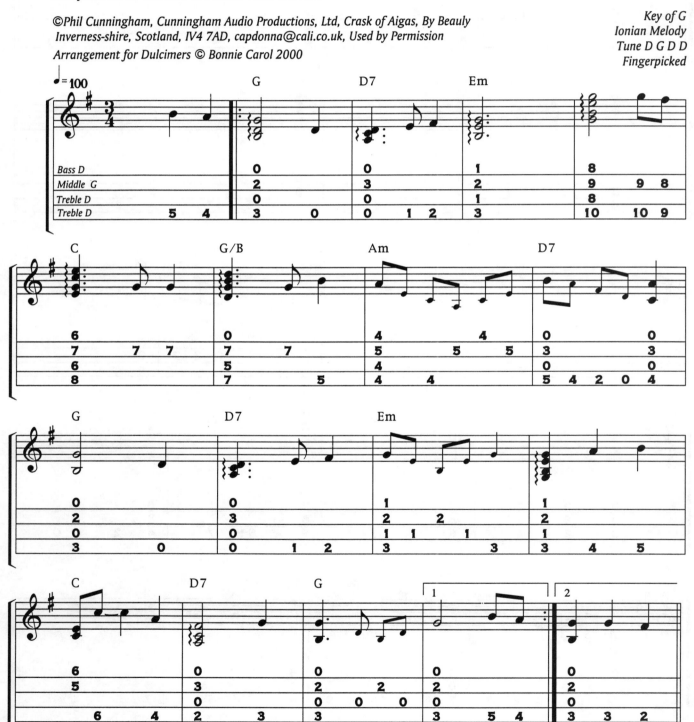

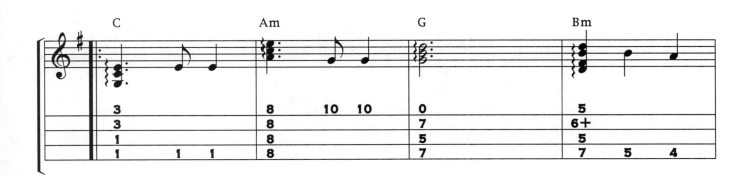

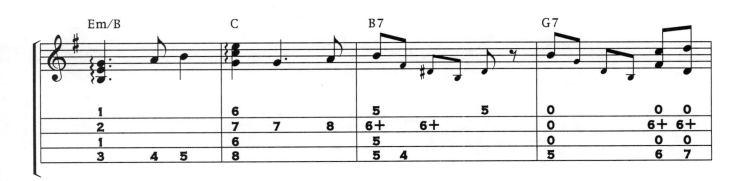

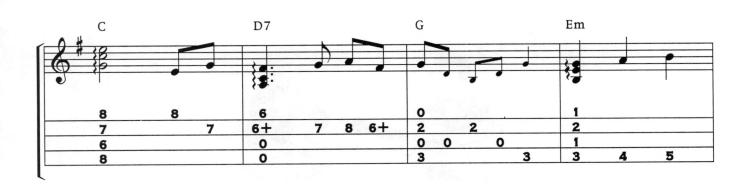

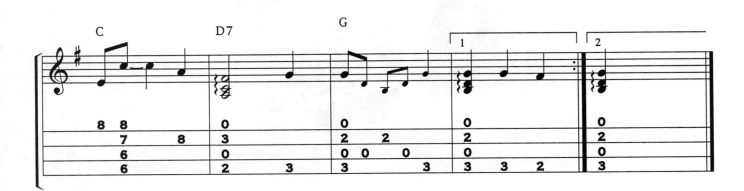

Bonnie@BonnieCarol.com • www.BonnieCarol.com • (303) 258-7763 • 15 Sherwood Road • Nederland, Colorado 80466

Alphabetical Index of Songs

(*4) Arrangements for four equidistant strings

Dulcimer pioneer, Bonnie Carol, has been found everywhere there are dulcimers since 1971. Her sweet music has filled concert halls from New York to Nicaragua, and she was the first teacher for many of today's dulcimer stars. As a multi-instrumentalist herself, she has always promoted the creation of communities of musicians playing together on all sorts of instruments featuring all sorts of music. Her latest two publications are (1) this book of arrangements of favorite to obscure jam session tunes arranged for both hammered and fretted dulcimers and (2) a collection of Latin American music arranged for hammered and fretted dulcimers.

Bonnie has professional credentials that are some of the most complete in the country. She has produced, recorded and distributed five recordings of her music on which she played the majority of the instruments, and has put her knowledge of traditional music and dulcimers into the five books she has authored. She has won or placed in most of the dulcimer contests in the nation. In her classes and workshops she can turn a dulcimer into a magical ally in the hands of the newest beginner or most seasoned musician. Bonnie's latest project is organizing musical river trips on the desert rivers of the great American Southwest. www.BonnieCarol.com is where you can find more info about this.